1

Praise for the Budgetnista

Evita Turquoise Robinson
1 hr · 🛪

Tiffany TheBudgetnista Aliche just changed my life!! Book this woman. Get her book. Follow her site. Take her out to lunch. Do something...but book her to help with any finance issues you have. Http://thebudgetnista.com

Unlike · Comment · Share

DrAlissa Dawn Gardenhire ▸ **Tiffany TheBudgetnista Aliche**
30 mins · 🌐

Tiffany TheBudgetnista Aliche Thank you for everything. I'm more knowledgable and inspired beyond belief. Thank you!

Unlike · Comment

De'Nita Moss ▸ **Tiffany TheBudgetnista Aliche**
5 mins · 🌐

Tiffany, your online presence is simply spectacular. Thank you for your consistency and reaching out with helpful information; beyond mere money. What an awesome example you are (for the entrepreneur or not), thanks!

Like · Comment · Share

Howard Quanita ▸ **Tiffany TheBudgetnista Aliche**
35 minutes ago near New York, NY 🌐

Hey Tiff.... As close as I am to being debt free. I'm off to the Beautiful Island of the🛪🛪🛪🛪🛪Bahamas paid in full (cash) no travel bill to think about later. I owe it all to you and the 6 week classes I took!!

Praise for the Budgetnista

Dori Le Grand-Christmas
16 hrs ·

Tiffany TheBudgetnista Aliche, you are my new go to guru for all things financial!!!! In just two short hours you have opened my eyes to the errors of my ways and gave insightful tips on how to make a mends and fix my situation. I am hopeful that I can dig myself out of my "six foot deep" status and resurrect my financial standing. Just be warned that I may stalk you!!! Lol thank you and Style Haven for allowing this informative session to transpire

Unlike · Comment · Share

Tiffany,
Thank you so much for launching this project. Thank you for the useful advice and encouragement. Thank you for addressing the needs of women everywhere to be financially solvent and independent. Thank you for what you are doing to impact our community. You are greatly appreciated.

As a divorced, single mother of two in my mid 30's, I am in the worst financial shape I have ever been in. It seems nearly impossible to keep above water and establish a savings. Though I am gainfully employed and currently sharing a residence with my parents, having "enough" seems a long way off.

I look forward to successfully changing my behaviors to establish habits that will result in long-term financial success not only for myself, but for my children as well. Thank you for doing this for women like me and women who are facing even greater challenges or none at all. You are a Godsend and a blessing.

Thank you from the bottom of my heart,

Praise for the One Week Budget

☆☆☆☆☆ **Finally - A Practical guide With Realistic Goals and an easy process!!!**, November 8, 2013

By **Gospel Chick** - See all my reviews

Verified Purchase (What's this?)

This review is from: **The One Week Budget: Learn to Create Your Money Management System in 7 Days or Less! (Kindle Edition)**

After years of attempting to pay down my debt, "The One Week Budget" came along with practical steps to not only pay down debt, but to SAVE as well. This is a must read! The Budgetnista walks you through each part of the process and shares her personal testimony on how she was able to manage her finances through debt reduction and savings. Her wisdom is so practical that you will see immediate solutions and gain. When you complete your worksheet reality will set in but forge ahead anyway. When you begin to apply her principals you'll be able to go back to the worksheet and see how far you came. Best book on finance I've ever had...and I've had many. It's life changing!!!!

Help other customers find the most helpful reviews   Report abuse | Permalink

Was this review helpful to you? (Yes) (No)   ☐ Comment

☆☆☆☆☆ **Learn A Budget, On a Budget**, July 5, 2013

By **IvyLaArtista™ "Creatively Inspired,"** (Atlanta, GA) - See all my reviews

Verified Purchase (What's this?)

This review is from: **The One Week Budget: Learn to Create Your Money Management System in 7 Days or Less! (Kindle Edition)**

So, if you are SERIOUS about getting your money in order, then two things you want to conserve: time and money. Those are two things that I don't have to waste. It seems like several budgeting books are overly complicated and padded with extra data and information that I couldn't really use. What I like about the book is that it is an easy read, yet practical. It doesn't take long to get started on implementing it into your life. It also is an awesome price for how much life value you will get from it. I didn't waste time or money on this book. I exponentially gained both and also received life principles that will help me to achieve my goals as a woman and entrepreneur. I recommend it to those who are intimidated by the word "budget". Go ahead...get started!

Help other customers find the most helpful reviews   Report abuse | Permalink

Was this review helpful to you? (Yes) (No)   ☐ Comment

☆☆☆☆☆ **Worth its Weight in Gold**, April 3, 2014

By **Amoi Holmes** - See all my reviews

This review is from: **The One Week Budget: Learn to Create Your Money Management System in 7 Days or Less! (Kindle Edition)**

This is a very simple a straightforward guide to managing your budget. It's is very simple and fun to read as the author is funny and full of personality. Once I was done reading it, I wished I had such a succinct guide when I was going into college. As much as I thought I knew how to save and budget back then, I found that I DID NOT!

I can honestly say that implementing the principles shared in this book, I have become better at saving and I can accurately gauge what I can spend on things that I love without feeling guilty about it or going overboard. If you lack discipline, this can definitely help if you follow the steps. Because you will be able to see where every cent of your money is going, you'll be able to make some wiser decisions when deciding where to put your money and what to spend it on.

I also think it's the perfect give for any student going off to college to set him/her up for success.

For mother, Sylvia. You taught me that money is a tool not a goal.
Thank you for showing me how to *LIVE RICHER.*

Let's get to know each other.

Hi. I'm Tiffany. Welcome to the beginning of your new financial journey. Are you finally ready to live a richer life? Well of course you are-- you're here!

To LIVE RICHER means to purposefully and passionately design and live your life. The purpose of the LIVE RICHER Challenge is to teach you how to use your finances as a tool to achieve that life.

Although I grew up in a household where financial education was taught regularly, I haven't always made the best choices with my money.

Tiffany's Financial Fiascos

1. At age 24, I took a $20,000 cash advance from my credit card and invested it with a "friend." This genius move landed me in $35,000 worth of debt a few months later.

2. At age 26, I bought my first home... right before the housing bubble burst. The value of my $220,000 condo declined to $150,000 in less than a year.

3. At age 30, as a result of losing my job (during the Recession) and being unable to keep up with my bills, the 802 credit score I once enjoyed quickly plummeted to 574.

Pretty bad, huh? Once I adopted my LIVE RICHER lifestyle, I was able to pay off my credit card debt in two and a half years, make peace with my mortgage lender, and raise my credit score almost 200 points in two years. I've even been able to travel to over 20 countries within the last few years.

Now I use the solutions that helped me during my Financial Fiascos as a tool to guide people like you, who want to do the same.

In 2008, I started "The Budgetnista," an award-winning professional and educational services firm. As "The Budgetnista," I'm a spokesperson who speaks, writes, and creates financial education products and services that include seminars, workshops, curricula, and trainings.

I've also written a bestselling book entitled, *The One Week Budget* (a #1 Amazon bestseller), which teaches readers how to budget their income and automate the process over a period of just seven days.

You can learn more about The Budgetnista at www.thebudgetnista.com.

Why do the challenge?

Enough about me. Let's talk about why you need to do this challenge. Have you ever asked yourself any of these questions?

1. How do you do a budget?
2. What's the best way to save?
3. How will I pay off my debt?
4. Do I have the right insurance?
5. How can I raise my credit score?
6. How do I get started investing?

Great! This challenge will answer all of these questions, plus more! I even promise to do so in a way that's easy to understand and implement. Just think — in 36 days you'll be able to accomplish many of the financial goals you've been working on for years.

HOW TO READ THIS BOOK

Are you ready to get on track financially? Good, because I'm determined to get you in fit, financial shape.

I've created this 36-day, LIVE RICHER Challenge to help you.

How it works:
Each day I'll assign an Easy Financial Task designed to help you get and stay on the road to financial freedom.

The daily tasks will focus on the money theme of the week. The weekly themes for the LIVE RICHER Challenge are:

Week 1: Money Mindset
Week 2: Budgeting & Saving
Week 3: Debt
Week 4: Credit
Week 5: Insurance & Investing
Final Day: LIVE RICHER

How to guarantee your success:
- Every morning read and commit to doing your Easy Financial Task.

- Perform the task. Don't worry, it won't be hard.

- Get accountability partners. One of the best ways to guarantee your success is to do the challenge with a group or at least with one other person. It will help to keep you motivated. You might even consider creating a LIVE RICHER team at work, among your friends, and within your family.

- Share your experiences with me, ask questions, and leave comments via social media.

You can find me online here...

The Budgetnista Blog: thebudgetnistablog.com

Twitter & Instagram: @TheBudgetnista

Facebook: The Budgetnista

I have created so many awesome resources for you that they couldn't all fit in this book so I've created a site where you can access them for free – www.livericherchallenge.com.

LIVE RICHER
 Tiffany "The Budgetnista" Aliche

Table of Contents

Table of Contents

WEEK 1: MONEY MINDSET

THIS WEEK'S GOAL:

To completely overhaul the way you think about your money by changing your Money Mindset.

Live Richer Challenge
Day 1: Financial Goals

Week 1: Money Mindset

Today's Easy Financial Task: Identify, write down, and share your goals.

How to rock this task:
- List no more than three of your personal financial goals
- Be specific
- Write down your goals & post them where you can see them daily
- Share them (tell me, tell a friend...tell someone)

This week we'll be focused on your Money Mindset. Remember, it doesn't matter how much money you have or make if you aren't capable of keeping it.

If you're to be rich, it's important that we get you thinking rich...

On the first day of our LIVE RICHER Challenge, I want you to identify your specific financial goals (Ex: "I want to save $2000 in four months"), write them down, place them somewhere you can see them daily, and share them with someone you trust.

Your goals should answer these three questions:
1 *What? (Ex: "I will save $1000")*
2 *When? (Ex: "by March 1st")*
3 *How? (Ex: "I will reduce my cable plan and bring my lunch to work instead of buying it.")*

Now is the time to pick an accountability partner(s). I suggest picking someone or organizing a group of people who want to do the challenge as well.

Don't forget, I'm also a resource to you and have formed a group online where you can join a community of people who are all working toward similar goals. You can find us at: www.livericherchallenge.com.

Back to today's task...

This task is important because it will help you to define the steps you'll need to take to accomplish your specific financial goals.

The why...
- Identifying and writing down your goals will give them power.
- Placing them somewhere visible will serve as a constant reminder.
- Sharing them will help to hold you accountable.

Ready? Set? Go! Write them down and share, share, share!

I look forward to the next 35 frugal, fun days with you.

My personal finance goals are...

_____

_____

_____

_____

_____

_____

_____

_____

_____

_____

_____

_____

Live Richer Challenge
Day 2: The Richest Man

Week 1: Money Mindset

Today's Easy Financial Task: Read "Seven Cures for a Lean Purse."

How to rock this task:
- Find *The Richest Man in Babylon (book)*
- Read the third story: "Seven Cures for a Lean Purse."
- Share your favorite "cure" with me and your accountability partners. Also share how you'll use this "cure" to grow wealth.

You've made it to Day 2. Congratulations!

As you know, this week we're focused on Money Mindset. This next task will really help to get you ready.

One of the best ways to correct a poverty mindset is to reset it with correct information. For today's task, I want you to read the third short story from one of my favorite financial books, *The Richest Man in Babylon.*

The simple principles in this book by George Clason can transform the way you look at your money forever! Written as eight stories in parable form, this quick read will have you living richer before you know it.

Although the whole book is awesome, I just want you to focus on one story for today, "Seven Cures For a Lean Purse."

Use your lunch break, when you're on the cardio-machine today at the gym, the time right before you go to bed, or whenever you get a chance, and read this story... **today.** The principles in *this* book, especially this story, will change your Money Mindset if you allow it to.

There are a number of free .pdf versions of this book online. Use your favorite search engine and start reading.

After reading this story, it's even more important that you reflect on the Seven Cures and how you can and will apply at least one to your life now.

Pick one of the seven "cures" and share how you will use it to reset yourself to a wealth-building Money Mindset.

Share with your accountability partner or group and share with me as well.

Find me here:

twitter / instagram: @thebudgetnista
Facebook: The Budgetnista
Forum: www.livericherchallenge.com (go to the website and request to join the LIVE RICHER forum.)

My favorite financial cure is...

_____

_____

_____

_____

_____

_____

_____

_____

_____

_____

_____

_____

Live Richer Challenge
Day 3: Essential Spending

Week 1: Money Mindset

Today's Easy Financial Task: Only buy what's necessary today.

How to rock this task:
- Only buy your **needs** today.
- No luxuries. For example, no coffee, snacks, soda, car wash, food that's not necessary, etc. (Yes, I said no coffee...just for today. However, you can bring it from home).
- Write down every time you were going to spend money and at the end of the day, add up how much you saved and share the amount with your accountability partners.

Today is our first video task. Yay! Visit www.livericherchallenge.com (Day 3 Essential Spending) to watch how to make today's task work for you. Share how much you saved with me in the video comment section.

The purpose of this task is to get you to see how much you spend daily on things that don't mean much. If you want to get your pockets right, you first have to get your mind right.

I can't wait to hear about your savings!

Today I did not buy...

_____

_____

_____

_____

_____

Live Richer Challenge
Day 4: Money Bucket

Week 1: Money Mindset

Today's Easy Financial Task: Open up a Money Bucket.

How to rock this task:
- Use www.MagnifyMoney.com to help you find a **free**, no fee, Savings/Money Market Account (MMA).
- Choose the free account that also gives the most interest.
- Transfer the money you saved from yesterday's task to your new account.

Today's Easy Financial Task is to open up a Money Bucket Account. What's a Money Bucket Account?

Picture this...

Days after it rains, you'd never know...Why? The reason is that the ground soaks up the water soon after a storm. You, my friend, are like the ground, and when it "rains" money (aka payday), you too soak up the water (your funds).

The only way to keep some of the rain is to put out a bucket. An *online-only* Savings or Money Market Account (MMA) is the perfect Money Bucket.

Why it works:
- It's FREE
- It takes 2-5 business days to transfer your money back into your current bank account. This mandatory wait will stop your impulse spending with savings. Make sure not to open a checking account at the same bank where you have your Money Buckets. If you do, you'll be able to make faster transfers and use your debit card to spend your savings, and that's not good.
- It makes your money inconvenient. This is the best strategy to curb unplanned spending.
- You can transfer $5 just as easily as $500.

The purpose of this task is to get you to see how easy it is to save. Many of us have the mindset that saving is hard, but it doesn't have to be. Once you open your first Money Bucket, throw something in there once a week... no matter how small.

"How?" you ask. Do what you did yesterday during the LIVE RICHER Challenge, Day 3 task, and choose one "essential only" spending day a week and transfer what you save on that day to your new account. You'll be surprised how quickly the money adds up.

Take this step even further and go back to your Day 1 Easy Financial Task and choose one of your financial goals as a focus for your savings. Saving for something specific is the best way to stick to your savings plan.

Just in case you're unsure, here is what you should look for in an online account when looking on www.MagnifyMoney.com :

Bank Criteria:
- The most essential quality in a bank is that it is FDIC insured. This means that the Federal Government insures that your money in the bank is protected up to $250,000 per depositor, per insured bank.
- Choose the highest interest rate.
- The amount needed to open up an account should be $0 or as low as possible.
- There should be no fees associated with the account. Want to take today's task a step further?

Share the wealth and pass along Day 3's Easy Financial Task with someone who you know needs financial help.

I saved $_____in my Money Bucket today!

Live Richer Challenge
Day 5: Need it? > Love it? > Like it? > Want it?

Week 1: Money Mindset

Today's Easy Financial Task: Identify your priorities.

How to rock this task:
- Make a mental list of your *needs* (food, shelter, clothing, water, etc.)
- Choose two *loves* that you can commit to for the next six months
- Write down your *loves* and share them with your accountability partners

These are the four questions you should ask yourself before spending any money.

Do I...
1 Need it?
2 Love it?
3 Like it?
4 Want it?

Identify and take care of your *needs* first, ie: food, shelter, clothing (this doesn't include trendy must-haves), water, etc.

Next, identify, write down, and share no more than two *loves*. This is **very** important. We often neglect the things we *love*, in favor of our *likes* and *wants*, because *likes* and *wants* tend to cost less and take less patience to acquire.

Having trouble thinking of your *loves?* Answer this question - If you had Oprah's bank account, what would you do or what would you do more of? Choose two of these things and those are likely the *loves* of your life.

If we're to change our Money Mindset this week, it's important that we switch to one of a purposeful, passionate financial life.

Needs = purpose
Loves = passion

If you don't *need* it, or *love* it, then you should leave it.

Spending money on *likes* or wants, means you'll have less money for purchases that truly improve the quality of your life.

Need additional help or want to share your *loves* with me?

Find me here:
twitter & instagram: @thebudgetnista
Facebook: The Budgetnista
Forum: www.livericherchallenge.com

My *loves* are...

_____

_____

_____

_____

_____

_____

_____

_____

_____

_____

Live Richer Challenge
Day 6: Simple and Soon

Week 1: Money Mindset

Today's Easy Financial Task: Do something today.

How to rock this task:
- Choose one of your goals from Day 1 of the LIVE RICHER Challenge
- Do something easy today that will bring you one step closer to accomplishing that goal
- Share your "do something" task with your accountability partners

One of the biggest barriers to success is lack of action due to our inability to get over a mental hurdle.

If we want to achieve something big and significant in our lives – anything – it begins with discipline and repetition of positive behaviors over time.

The secret is: smaller steps over a long period of time will have a greater effect on our lives than bigger steps in a shorter period of time. The reason is that most of us cannot commit to these big, abnormal acts for long, but we can do smaller, easier things consistently.

Example: Attempting to save $200/month when you've previously saved nothing, is much harder than taking the change out of your pocket every night and putting it in a jar to save for later.

It's easier to commit to the small act of saving change. In the long run, that small act will make all the difference, because you'll actually do it, rather than get frustrated when you can't meet a larger goal.

I want to leave you with this story: Actor Will Smith was 11 years old when his father asked him and his brother to rebuild a brick wall that had been torn down. Naturally, Will and his brother protested and said it was "impossible," but his father insisted and the boys got to work. A year and a half later, the wall was complete and Will and his brother learned a valuable lesson.

Will shared this lesson in an interview: "You don't set out to build a wall. You don't say, 'I'm going to build the biggest, baddest, greatest wall that's ever been built.' You don't start there. You say, 'I'm going to lay this brick as perfectly as a brick can be laid.' You do that every single day... and soon you have a wall."

You can watch this motivating interview at www.livericherchallenege.com under Day 6: Simple and Soon

I will do something today. Today I will...

Live Richer Challenge
Day 7: Review, Reflect, Relax

Week 1: Money Mindset

Today's Easy Financial Task: Review, Reflect, Relax.

How to rock this task:
- *Review* this week's six LIVE RICHER Challenge tasks
- *Reflect* on the changes you've made and your new Money Mindset
- *Relax.* Tomorrow we start Week 2: Budgeting & Saving

Round of applause!

You've completed the first week of the LIVE RICHER Challenge.

Take this day to review, reflect, and relax.

Share what you've learned and how you feel about the process with me and your accountability partners.

Don't forget...

It's great to be helped, but it's even greater to use what you've been given to help someone else.

Share the wealth and pass the LIVE RICHER Challenge along to someone you know who is struggling to master their money.

Week 1: Money Mindset Recap Checklist

○ **Day 1:** Easy Financial Task: Identify, write down, and share your goals

○ **Day 2:** Easy Financial Task: Read "Seven Cures for a Lean Purse"

○ **Day 3:** Easy Financial Task: Only buy what's necessary today

○ **Day 4:** Easy Financial Task: Open up a Money Bucket

○ **Day 5:** Easy Financial Task: Identify your priorities

○ **Day 6:** Easy Financial Task: Do something today

○ **Day 7:** Easy Financial Task: Review, Reflect, Relax

Week 1 Reflections

_____

_____

_____

_____

_____

_____

_____

_____

_____

_____

WEEK 2: BUDGETING & SAVINGS

THIS WEEK'S GOAL:

To create a budget, find ways to decrease your expenses, and contribute more to savings.

Live Richer Challenge
Day 8: *The One Week Budget*

Week 1: Money Mindset

Today's Easy Financial Task: Read *The One Week Budget* (Day 1).

How to rock this task:
- Get Day 1 of *The One Week Budget* for free at www.livericherchallenge.com
- Read Day 1 (especially the Easy Action Steps/RECAP)

Woohoo! You've made it to the second week of the LIVE RICHER Challenge. Pat yourself on the back if you're flexible; give yourself a hug if you're not.

This is the most important week of the Challenge. Having a budget is the key to financial success. It's the critical step in your new financial journey.

Last week, we covered Money Mindset, so I hope your mind is right, because this week we're tackling Budgeting & Saving.

ALL of your financial success rests upon your ability to budget. I repeat... all of your financial success rests upon your ability to properly budget your money.

To get started, go to www.livericherchallenge.com (Day 8: The One Week Budget) and claim your free copy of Day 1 of my bestselling book, *The One Week Budget.*

If you have time, please read all of Day 1 (it's not long, I promise). If you don't have time, you can read the Easy Action Steps from Day 1 at www. livericherchallenge.com *The One Week Budget*. Get excited! Tomorrow you'll have a chance to create your budget and put what you've learned today to good use.

Live Richer Challenge
Day 9: Your Money List

Week 2: Budgeting & Saving

Today's Easy Financial Task: Create your Money List

How to Rock This Task:
- List everything you spend money on
- Write down how much you spend *monthly* on each expense on your Money List
- Add up your Money List and subtract the amount from your *monthly* take-home pay
- Use The One Week Budget (Day 1) to help you fill out your Money List

Today's task will be **the most important task of the challenge.** Today, you'll create your Money List — a basic budget.

The reason why this task is so critical is that if *you* change your budget, *you* change your life.

Having a budget has enabled me to totally design my life. I now:

- Work for myself
- Travel the world (for much less than you'd think)
- LIVE RICHER: a purposeful, passionate life

You might be feeling a little overwhelmed after this task, but don't worry, that's normal. The rest of the challenge is going to teach you how to take control of your finances and change your results. Remember, I'll be here with you every step of the way.

Here's a blank Money List Template you can use to complete today's task. You can also download a free digital copy at www.li;velricherchallenge.com under Day 9: Your Money List.

My Money List

NAME OF EXPENSE	CURRENT MONTHLY AMOUNT	REDUCED MONTHLY AMOUNT	DUE DATE
MONTHLY TAKE HOME PAY			
MONTHLY SPENDING			
		subtract	
SAVINGS (take home pay - total spending)			
TOTAL			
SAVINGS (Take Home Pay - Total Spending)			

Live Richer Challenge
Day 10: Your Spending

Week 2: Budgeting & Saving

Today's Easy Financial Task: Reduce your spending.

How to rock this task:
- Take out your Money List
- Call the providers of the services you pay for on your Money List and ask for a discount
- Commit to saving on other expenses from your Money List
- Update your Money List with your new savings by filling out the REDUCED MONTHLY AMOUNT column

Now that you finally have a Money List (budget), it's time to find some savings.

For today's task, take out your Money List and go line item by line item and decide how much money you think you can squeeze from things like groceries, grooming, entertainment, eating out, transportation etc. Remember, no amount is too small.

Then, call the service providers on your list, like your car insurance, lenders, cable, utilities, cell phone companies etc. and ask them for a discount. Yup! I said it. Ask them if you can pay less...

A Success Story:

One of my clients asked her car insurance company for a discount and was able to save $450/month! How? Apparently her insurance company had all of these discounts that they never applied to the cars on her account. She had been with them for 10+ years and had never asked. When she said she was going to leave them for another company, they "magically" found the discounts.

You may not save as much as she did, but you will likely be able to save *something* and that's awesome too.

Feeling nervous about making this type of call? No worries, here's a script to help you.

The Script:

"Hello, my name is_____and I've been a loyal customer for_____ years. I was reviewing my bill from your agency and due to financial constraints, I'm not able to continue paying this amount. I want to remain a customer; is there something you can do to help me? "

Script Tips:

- Be pleasant. I cannot stress this enough. The person on the phone has way more power than you know. They are able to do a lot for you, and will only do so based upon how you treat them. So be nice. Ask how their day is going; say thank you and that you appreciate their help, etc.
- Be persistent. Just because one person says no, that doesn't mean the next one will. Hang-up and try again.
- Do a little research. Find out some of their competitors' rates and use that politely against them. That's how my client was able to save $450/month after a phone call to her car insurance company.
- Be prepared to leave. If you really can't afford the service any longer, you might have to cancel it. If you keep getting no's, ask to be transferred to their *Retention Department.*

The Retention Department is the service provider's last chance to offer you some help. If they don't, you may have to let them go. I canceled my cable several years ago after getting too many no's. It was the best decision, because now I use that money to go on vacations instead.

Don't forget to update yesterday's Money List with your new savings by filling out the REDUCED MONTHLY AMOUNT column. I look forward to hearing your savings success stories. Share them with me here:

twitter & Instagram: @thebudgetnista
Facebook: The Budgetnista
Forum: www.livericherchallenge.com

Live Richer Challenge
Day 11: Defining Dollars

Week 2: Budgeting & Saving

Easy Financial Task 11: Open multiple accounts

How to Rock This Task:
- Open separate bank accounts for deposits, bills, and savings

Today we have another video. Yay! Visit www.livericherchallenge.com (Day 11: Defining Dollars) to learn more about the three types of accounts you'll need to complete this task.

Let's get started...

Did you know that separating your money is a useful management tool to keep you on financial track? Having all of your money in one account can create confusion about what money is allocated for what purpose. Using different accounts for your specific financial goals is a great way to organize your money.

The accounts you should have are:

Deposit Account: A checking account where all of the money you make is deposited. It's attached to your debit card.

Bills Account: A checking account where you transfer your money for bills.

Savings/Money Market Account(s): An online-only savings account(s) where you put your emergency savings and money for other savings goals. These are your Money Buckets from Day 4. You can and should have multiple Savings Accounts for different things (ex: car, home, travel etc.)

You probably already have a Deposit Account; it's your current checking account that you're regularly using. If you don't have one, go to www.magnifymoney.com and find the best bank or credit union and open one. I also suggest that you sign up for direct deposit at work. This way, the money you receive from your job(s) gets sent directly to your account.

Open your Bills Account at the same bank as your Deposit Account, because you will be transferring your bill money between the two accounts, and having them both at the same bank will make transfers super easy. Make sure that the bank has an online bill-pay option. Also, do not connect a debit card to your Bills Account, because you don't want to accidentally (ummm, on purpose) spend your bill money when you swipe your debit card.

Open up your Savings/Money Market Account(s) (see Easy Financial Task 4 for the steps).

You might be asking : "Why do I have to open up another Savings Account?"

I believe that for each financial goal you have, you should open a free, online-only Savings Account, a Money Bucket. Having a separate account for each goal will help you to quickly identify how close you are to accomplishing each goal.

Stashing your money in an online-only Savings Account will help to stop impulse spending. It takes 2-5 business days for the money you've saved to be transferred from your online accounts to your regular bank account. Waiting for your money will deter you from spending it outside of your goal(s).

Your Grandma used to use the envelope system. Multiple accounts is the updated version. Some financial tools are tried and true.

Live Richer Challenge
Day 12: Automation

Week 2: Budgeting & Saving

Today's Easy Financial Task: Begin to automate.

How to rock this task:
- Automate transfers to your Savings Account(s)
- Automate transfers to your Bills Account
- Automate your bill payments

By now you should already have a budget and multiple accounts. Today we automate!

Automation is the new discipline. By taking out the "flawed" human element, aka *you*, you're more likely to stick to your budget. I've automated everything: bills, savings, investing, even giving to charity.

Begin by automating transfers to your Bills and Savings Accounts. Then, automate your bill payments, to insure you're never late again (assuming you have the money available in your Bills Account).

I would *not* suggest that you allow companies in to take their payments. Instead, use your bank's free, online bill-pay option and make your bill payments that way.

You can even automate payments to small companies and individuals. If the bank can't wire the money, they'll simply cut a check and mail it.

No more excuses. You have all the tools you need to successfully budget your money.

Make sure to check in with your accountability partners. Are they saving more? Have they opened up their accounts? Have they automated their expenses?

Live Richer Challenge
Day 13: Allowance

Week 2: Budgeting & Saving

Today's Easy Financial Task: Give yourself an allowance.

How to rock this task:
- Identify the cash expenses on your Money List (ex. groceries, entertainment, grooming, etc.)
- Add your monthly cash expenses up and divide them by four (weeks)
- Set aside that amount as your weekly allowance and use it (preferably as cash)

You should already have a budget (your Money List). Next, identify your cash expenses. These are things that are not bills or utilities. Cash expenses are items that you can and probably should pay for with cash, like eating out, grooming, and daily coffees. Add up your monthly cash expenses, and then divide the amount by four weeks. This new number is your weekly allowance.

You can spend your allowance in two ways:
- Leave it in your Deposit Account (see Day 11), and spend it using your debit card
- Withdraw your allowance every week and use it as cash

Cash is still Queen. It is almost always best to pay cash versus a credit or debit card because it reduces your likelihood of overdrafting and keeps you more aware of how much you are actually spending.

There is evidence that shows that consumers spend 18% more on average when using a credit card vs. cash (JW PerkStreet Financial). When you use your debit card or credit card to purchase something, oftentimes the money does not feel real, so you end up spending more. When you pay with cash, you actually see and feel your money leaving your grasp. It is a painful thing sometimes, because with cash, you know your money is going to someone else, therefore prompting you to spend less.

My cash expenses are...

Live Richer Challenge
Day 14: Review, Reflect, Relax

Week 2: Budgeting & Saving

Today's Easy Financial Task: Review, Reflect, Relax.

How to rock this task:
- *Review* this week's six LIVE RICHER Challenge tasks
- *Reflect* on the changes you've made and your new budgeting and savings plan
- *Relax.* Tomorrow we start Week 3: Debt

Yes! Look at YOU! You've completed the second week of the LIVE RICHER Challenge!

Break-day. All I want you to do today is: Review, Reflect, and Relax. Today is also a great day to catch up on any of the tasks you've missed.

Share what you've learned over the last two weeks with me and your accountability partners. Don't forget, when you teach you learn twice. Use these daily tasks to help someone else who needs help getting on financial track.

Week 2: Budgeting & Saving Recap Checklist

○ **Day 8:** Easy Financial Task: Read The One Week Budget (Day 1)

○ **Day 9:** Easy Financial Task: Create your Money List

○ **Day 10:** Easy Financial Task: Reduce your spending

○ **Day 11:** Easy Financial Task: Open multiple accounts

○ **Day 12:** Easy Financial Task: Begin to automate

○ **Day 13:** Easy Financial Task: Give yourself an allowance

○ **Day 14:** Easy Financial Task: Review, Reflect, Relax

Week 2 Reflections

_____

_____

_____

_____

_____

_____

_____

_____

WEEK 3: DEBT

THIS WEEK'S GOAL:

To identify and verify your debts and understand your rights. To create a debt repayment plan and earmark money for repayment.

Live Richer Challenge
Day 15: Debt List

Week 3: Debt

Today's Easy Financial Task: Make a list of your debt (expenses with a balance)

How to rock this task :
- Use www.CreditKarma.com to help you find the debt you "forgot" (don't worry, it's free)
- Use the "My Debt List" template to list your debt and its name, balance, minimum payment, etc.

This is the week you may have been waiting for... Debt Week! By the end of this week you'll have an awesome, automated, Debt-Pay-Down plan.

Are you ready? Get set. Let's go!

You may be wondering, "What should I put on My Debt List?" Answer: Include anything with a balance. (Ex. student loans, credit cards, money you owe to a friend or family member, car note, late payments, anything that you have to pay off.)

Use www.CreditKarma.com to help you find some of the debt you may have forgotten about.

Use this My Debt List template to help you complete today's task. You can also download a free, digital copy at www.livericherchallenge.com under Day 15: Debt List.

My Debt List
(NOTE: List debt lowest to highest)

NAME OF DEBT	TOTAL AMT. OWED	MIN. MONTHLY PMT.	INTEREST RATE	DUE DATE	STATUS

Live Richer Challenge
Day 16: Find Money

Week 3: Debt

Today's Easy Financial Task: Find money to pay down your debt

How to Rock This Task:
- Take out your Money List from Day 9
- Write down how much money you saved on Day 10
- Decide how much of that monthly savings will go towards your Debt-Pay-Down-Plan

So, let's get started...

As you know, this is Week 3 and we're tackling your debt. Yesterday, I had you make a list of all your debt and its terms.

All I want you to do today is to use your Money List to figure out how much money you can allocate to pay down your debt each month. Now do you see why a physical budget is so important?

Note: Some of the extra monthly money you found during Day 10 (Reduce Your Spending), should *still* be earmarked for savings, but some of it should be set aside for debt too. If you have debt, paying it down and saving should happen simultaneously.

Once you've identified how much money each month can go toward debt, don't do anything yet. I just need you to make a note of the amount. Tomorrow I will show you how you'll use the extra money to activate your Budgetnista Debt-Pay-Down-Plan.

How much did you decide to allocate for debt? Let me know. Tell your accountability partner. Make a note of it.

I will allocate $_____ of my savings to pay down my debt.

Live Richer Challenge
Day 17: Debt Repayment

Week 3: Debt

Today's Easy Financial Task: Start your Debt-Pay-Down-Plan

How to Rock This Task :
- Take out your completed My Debt List from Day 15
- Make note of the amount of money you've allocated for debt from yesterday's task
- Work through the Budgetnista Debt-Pay-Down-Plan

Today we have another video. Woohoo! Visit www.livericherchallenge.com (Day 17: Debt Repayment), to watch how to make today's task work for you.

Before you start paying down your debt, let's take care of your credit cards with high interest rates. Because I suggest that you pay off your debt with the lowest balances first, you may worry about neglecting your credit cards with high interest rates. There are a couple ways to get your interest rates down.

1) Call your credit card company(ies) and negotiate for lower rates. The better your credit, the more likely they are to work with you.

2) Transfer the balance of your higher interest rate credit card(s) onto a lower interest rate card(s).

Wondering how to do a balance transfer? Here's how:

Go to www.magnifymoney.com and search for a balance transfer card. Look for a card that offers a 0% interest rate for at least six months and the lowest transfer fee available. Take note: when doing a balance transfer, credit card companies will often charge you a fee - about 3% of the total balance you're transferring.

FYI: Sometimes credit card companies run a special where you can transfer your balance without a fee. That's the type of deal you're looking for on www.magnifymoney.com. Also, note that getting a new card will result in an inquiry that stays on your credit report for two years and can temporarily lower your credit score. (I share more about this on Day 24)

Once you locate a card you're interested in, call the company and ask:
- How long will the 0% introductory rate last?
- What will my rate be after the introductory rate expires?
- How much is the transfer fee?
- What happens if I'm late with a payment?
- Is there any fine print that I should know about?

Once you've taken care of your credit cards with high interest rates, you can then work on systematically paying off your debt.

Here's the step-by-step guide to The Budgetnista Debt-Pay-Down-Plan:

1) List all of your debt from lowest to highest.

2) Figure out how much money you can squeeze from your budget for your Debt-Pay-Down-Plan, Day 16 task. Remember, you should still be saving while paying off debt..

3) **Pay only the minimum amount required on all your debt, with the exception of the first debt on your list.** This should be the card or debt with the lowest amount owed.

Note: Why should you pay off your debt from lowest to highest balances vs. highest to lowest interest rates? Paying off your debt with the lowest balance first will give you the early success and motivation you'll need to stick to your Debt-Pay-Down-Plan. If you use the tips I gave you earlier on reducing your interest rates, they won't be such a large factor in your repayment plan.

4) Pay the minimum and the money you squeezed from your budget (Day 16) toward the first debt on your list.

5. Automate the payments. This will leave you with less work and tallying to do each month. Make sure you automate the payments to reflect how many months it will take to pay down whatever main debt you are focused on paying off. Then reset your automation when you move on to the next debt.

6. Use UM (Unexpected Money) to help pay down the main debt you're focused on. You'd know what UM was if you watched this week's video.... I'm just saying.

7. After paying off the first credit card, apply ALL the money you used each month to pay off that card and put it towards the next card (second lowest debt) on your list. This means that the minimum amount from the first card, the minimum from the second, and the extra money that you found in your budget, will be applied toward the next debt on your list.

8. Automate this new payment. Remember: doing this will help you stick to your strategy.

9. Use UM to help pay down this card.

10. Pay off the second card, then transfer ALL of the money you were paying each month to the second card and apply it towards the third card, along with its minimum (similar to step 7).

I suggest you continue this cycle until you pay off *all* of your credit card debt. Once you are credit card debt free, use this system to pay off the rest of your debt and finance your savings, retirement, and investment goals.

And *that* is how you get out of debt faster than you ever imagined. *Drops mike and sashays away.*

If you're still a little confused, no worries! Watch the Debt-Pay-Down-Plan video on www.livericherchallenge.com (Day 17: Debt Repayment) and I'll walk you through the steps.

If you have more questions, reach out to me!
twitter & instagram: @thebudgetnista
Facebook: The Budgetnista
Forum: www.livericherchallenge.com

Live Richer Challenge
Day 18: Verify Your Debt

Week 3: Debt

Today's Easy Financial Task: Call and verify your debt

How to Rock This Task:
- Reach out to your debt collectors or wait until they call again
- When speaking with your debt collectors, *do not* agree or admit to anything except your name and address
- Request a Debt Validation Letter verbally and in writing

Yesterday, I showed you step-by-step how to pay off your debt. Today, I'll show you how to find out if some of your debt is expired and can no longer be legally collected.

Here's how:

The next time a debt collector calls you, request a Debt Validation Letter verbally and in writing.

Why?
- Unless the collector is from the original company to whom you owed money, you never know who you're actually speaking with.
- Your debt may be what's called "Zombie Debt" and past the Statute of Limitations for collections. Every state allows debt collectors a certain number of years to use the legal avenues available to them to recoup their money from you.

In New Jersey (where I live), the Statute of Limitations on credit card debt is six years. That means that after six years of my (credit card) debt being inactive (the last time I made or promised to make a payment or used my card), the debt collector cannot legally collect from me. Many collectors will try to get you to renew the Statute of Limitations on expired debt by getting you to agree that you owe the debt and to make a payment, no matter how small.

This is why it's so important not to admit to anything or agree to a payment until you get your Debt Validation Letter. The letter will show you how long your debt has been inactive. If it's past the Statute of Limitations in your state : (Google your state's Statute of Limitations on debt), although you owe it, the collector cannot legally pursue you. A debt collector may still try to take you to court for "Zombie Debt," but if you have your Debt Validation Letter from them, it's your evidence that the debt has expired.

I'm not advocating that you don't pay what you owe. I just want you to focus on paying off current debt active within the last two years. Current debt has the biggest impact on your credit score, so paying it off will increase your score and help your credit report look better. After handling current debt, if you want to pay off old "Zombie Debt," then you should.

After verbally requesting your Debt Validation Letter, make sure to send your request via certified mail or via fax, for proof of receipt.

Get a free, Debt Validation Letter template at www.livericherchallenge.com under Day 18: Verify Your Debt.

Live Richer Challenge
Day 19: Stop the Calls

Week 3: Debt

Today's Easy Financial Task: Send Cease & Desist Letters

How to Rock This Task :
- Get your list of your debt collectors from your credit report. You can get a free report and score at www.creditkarma.com
- Use Google to find the mailing addresses for debt collectors who keep calling, or ask for their address or fax number the next time they call you
- Send a Cease & Desist Letter via certified mail or fax

Are you getting harassed by debt collectors? Did you know that if you ask them to stop calling you, they must? It's the law.

The best way to get a debt collector to stop calling you is to send them a Cease and Desist Letter via certified mail or fax. That's what I did when my mortgage company kept calling my parents and my sister's job asking for me.

I was once a classroom teacher and one day I lost my job when my school suddenly closed down. I called my mortgage company right away to work out a solution, because I could no longer afford my mortgage. Although I was in almost-daily contact with them, they still felt the need to try and shame me by calling my family asking for me. Each time they called a family member, I reached out and I told them that they could call me and supplied them with my number. This happened several times. The calls to my family persisted until I sent my mortgage company a Cease and Desist Letter via fax. After that, the calls stopped immediately.

Get the free template for the Cease and Desist Letter that I sent to my mortgage company at www.livericherchallenge.com under Day 19: Stop the Calls.

Tip: Make sure to list the number(s) that you want your creditors to stop calling, and supply them with the way you want to be contacted (email or mailing address).

Have your accountability partners done yesterday's task and requested a Debt Validation Letter? Have they prepared a Cease and Desist Letter? Now is a good time to check in on them.

Live Richer Challenge
Day 20: Your Rights

Week 3: Debt

Today's Easy Financial Task: Understand your rights

How to rock this task:
- There are a bunch of laws that protect you from law-breaking debt collectors
- These laws are called The Fair Debt Collections Practices Act (FDCPA)
- Learn your rights and review the FDCPA laws at www.ftc.gov

Did you know that there is a set of laws that protects you from debt collectors? Yes! Owing money does not give anyone the right to be abusive to you. Today, I want you to arm yourself with knowledge. Once you know what debt collectors are and are not allowed to do and say, you won't be afraid to pick up the phone again.

In fact, once you review the The Fair Debt Collections Practices Act laws, the next time a debt collector breaks one of them while interacting with you, say *"You've just violated The Fair Debt Collections Practices Act. If you continue to do so I will report you to my state Attorney General's office (**www.naag. org**) and the Federal Trade Commission (**www.ftc.gov**)."*

If your debt collector is stubborn and continues to break the law, research the web for a Debt Lawyer. A lawyer may be able to get the offending debt collection agency to pay you a fine and pay your lawyer's legal fees too!

Remember...

The purpose of the FDCPA: to eliminate abusive practices in the collection of consumer debts, to promote fair debt collection, and to provide consumers with an avenue for disputing and obtaining validation of debt information in order to ensure the information's accuracy.

(Thompson Hall Santi Cerny & Katkov | Aaron Hall)

Here are the laws in a nutshell from the government site, www.ftc.gov.

The FDCPA restricts debt collectors from engaging in conduct including the following:

• Contacting a third party who does not owe the debt, such as your relative, neighbor, or employer. Co-signers to the debt, however, may be contacted by the debt collector.

• Threatening to refer your account to an attorney, harm your credit rating, repossess or garnish, without actual intention of action on the threat. Please note that a debt collector may warn you of an actual impending intention to refer your case to an attorney or to report your debt to a credit agency. What they cannot do is use a false threat to try to intimidate you into paying.

• Making telephone calls at unreasonable times. The act defines unreasonable times as contact before 8:00 AM or after 9:00 PM, unless you have given the debt collector permission to contact you during those hours.

• Placing telephone calls to an inconvenient place. For example, contacting you at work in violation of a policy by your employer that is known to the debt collector or following a request by you that they not contact you at work. When placing a telephone call to you at work, informing your employer of the purpose of the call, unless first asked by the employer.

• Communicating with you if you notify a debt collector in writing that you refuse to pay a debt or that you wish the debt collector to cease further communication with you. The debt collector shall not communicate further with you with respect to such debt, except to advise you that the debt collector's further efforts are being terminated or that further specific action is being taken.

• Using obscenity, racial slurs, or insults.

- Sending letters which appear to have come from a court.

- Seeking collection fees or interest charges not permitted by your contract or by state law.

- Requesting post-dated checks with the intention to prosecute if they bounce.

- Suing in courts far removed from your place of residence.

- Making certain false representations in association with efforts to collect the debt, including the false claim that the person contacting you in relation to the debt is an attorney, falsely claiming to have started a lawsuit, using a false name, or using stationery that is designed to look like an official court or government communication.

- Using false claims to collect information about you, such as pretending to be conducting a survey.

- Threatening you with arrest if you do not pay the debt.

Helpful? I hope you feel protected against unsavory debt collectors now that you know that the FDCPA offers you protection.

If today's task has helped you, please share the wealth and pass it along to a friend or family member who's struggling with debt collectors too.

Live Richer Challenge
Day 21: Review, Reflect, Relax

Week 3: Debt

Today's Easy Financial Task: Review, Reflect, Relax

How to rock this task :
- *Review* this week's six LIVE RICHER Challenge tasks
- *Reflect* on the changes you've made and your new knowledge about debt
- *Relax.* Tomorrow we start Week 4's theme: Credit!

Congrats! It's already the end of Week 3 of the LIVE RICHER Challenge. We've fully covered Money Mindset, Budgeting & Savings, and now Debt.

It's time for another break-day. Today I want you to Review, Reflect, and Relax. It's also a great day to catch up on any of the tasks you still need to complete.

Feel free to share with me what you've learned by doing this challenge over the last three weeks.

Don't forget that sharing is caring. Share what you've learned with someone else who needs help getting on financial track and check in on your accountability partners.

Tomorrow begins Week 4 and it's all about credit.

Week 3: Debt Recap Checklist

○ **Day 15:** Easy Financial Task: Make a list of your debt (expenses with a balance)

○ **Day 16:** Easy Financial Task: Find money to pay down your debt

○ **Day 17:** Easy Financial Task: Start your Debt Repayment Plan

○ **Day 18:** Easy Financial Task: Call and verify your debt

○ **Day 19:** Easy Financial Task: Send Cease & Desist Letters

○ **Day 20:** Easy Financial Task: Understand your rights

○ **Day 21:** Easy Financial Task: Review, Reflect, Relax

Week 3 Reflections

_____

_____

_____

_____

_____

_____

_____

_____

_____

WEEK 4: CREDIT

THIS WEEK'S GOAL:

To learn how your credit score is calculated, how to get your score for free, and how to establish a plan for raising it.

Live Richer Challenge
Day 22: Credit Report

Week 4: Credit

Today's Easy Financial Task: Get your free credit report(s)

How to rock this task:
- Go to www.experian.com, www.transunion.com, and www.equifax.com
- Get your free credit reports

Hurray! You've made it to the Credit week! This week I'll show you how to get your free credit reports, how to clean up your report, and most importantly, how to dramatically raise your credit score in a relatively short period of time.

Let's get started! Did you know that you can get your credit report every year....for free? Yup! There are three main credit-reporting agencies, and each of them will give you your credit report once a year at no cost.

These agencies are:
Experian: 1-888- 397-3742 / www.experian.com
TransUnion: 1-800-888-4213 / www.transunion.com
Equifax: 1-800-685-1111 / www.equifax.com
So what are you waiting for? Go and get your credit reports!

Some people like to get them all at once, while others like to space them out and request a different one every three months. Whatever your preference is ... just make sure you get them.

Shocked about your credit report? Don't worry. I'm going to show you how to improve it in the next few days.

Live Richer Challenge
Day 23: Credit Score

Week 4: Credit

Today's Easy Financial Task: Get your free credit score(s) (not to be confused with your credit report)

How to Rock This Task :
- Go to www.creditkarma.com and sign up (it's free)
- Get your free credit score in minutes
- Get familiar with Credit Karma - it's an awesome site with a ton of resources

I'm pretty excited to share this week's tasks with you. Why? Because I'm going to show you how to raise your score as much as 100 points in 1 year!

Let's get started.
Today I want you to get your credit score. This is not to be confused with yesterday's task of getting your credit report.

Credit scores are usually $9 or more, but who wants to pay that? There are a couple of places where you can get a free credit score.

> **FYI: credit score ranges from 300 – 850**
> 751 – 850 Excellent
> 701 – 750 Good
> 641 – 700 Fair
> 581 – 641 Poor
> 300 – 580 Very Poor

1. www.CreditKarma.com: Not only does Credit Karma give you your TransUnion score and report for free, it educates you about your whole report in an easy-to-understand way.
2. www.CreditSesame.com: Credit Sesame enables you to view your Experian credit score and monitor important changes to your credit report.
3. Your bank: Many banks will give their customers their credit scores for free, so head to the closest bank branch and ask.

Remember: here are three main credit-reporting agencies: Experian, TransUnion, and Equifax. That means three reports and three scores.

Once you get your score, don't worry if it's low... in a couple of days I'll show you how to make it jump like Jordan!

Time to check in with your accountability partners. Have they gotten their credit reports and scores?

My Experian credit score is_____**date:**_____

My TransUnion credit score is_____**date:**_____

My Equifax credit score is_____**date:**_____

Live Richer Challenge
Day 24: Credit Calculations

Week 4: Credit

Today's Easy Financial Task: Learn how your credit score is calculated

How to Rock This Task :
- Learn the five components of your credit score and how much weight each component carries
- Identify which components are hurting and helping your credit score

Let's get this party started...
Today I'm going to show you the magic formula of how your credit score is calculated. There are five key components of a credit score and each component plays a weighted role in your financial future.

The five components are:
1. Inquiries: 10%
2. Type of debt: 10%
3. Length of credit history: 15%
4. Utilization: 30%
5. Payment history: 35%

1. Inquiries: 10%
An Inquiry happens when your credit report is looked into. Each time you **authorize** (usually by supplying your social security number), someone other than you access to your credit report, your score potentially goes down by 8-30 points. Sometimes, it is necessary to have your credit report pulled; for example, reports are requested when you apply for certain jobs, rent a car, get car insurance, open up a new credit card, or apply for a loan. Remember to be careful when allowing someone access to your credit. You may be unnecessarily sacrificing credit score points and inquiries that will stay on your report for two years.

Inquiry Example: Applying for a store card at the register in order to save 15% on your purchases.

Inquiry Tip: Did you know that Inquiries from store cards take the most points off of your credit score?

2. Type of Debt: 10%
The three main credit bureaus, Experian, TransUnion, and Equifax, like to see different types of debt. If all you have are student loans, you look like an inexperienced debtor who may not be able to handle other kinds of debt. I'm not suggesting that you get into debt for debt's sake. I just want you to be aware of what the credit bureaus look at when assigning you that all important number...your credit score.

Type of Debt Examples: Credit card, student loan, mortgage, car note, personal loan

Type of Debt Tip: If you're on the market for a mortgage, being great with credit cards won't help you much. Instead, get a notarized letter from your current landlord stating your on-time payment history and bring a copy of at least two years of bank statements to support the letter.

3. Length of Credit History: 15%
The longer you've had credit, the better. Be sure to keep that in mind when deciding whether or not to close a credit card. You may want to consider closing one of your newer cards instead. Your older cards are proof of a longer credit history. The length of your credit history is an average of all of your open credit accounts. Be careful of opening up too many new accounts because they will bring the length of your credit history down.

Length of Credit History Example: I've had my mortgage for 10 years, a credit card for 15 years, and another credit card for 5 years. My length of credit history is: 10+15+5 / 3 = 10 years.

Length of Credit History Tip: As awesome as it is to pay off a car loan, student loan, or mortgage, you may temporarily lose some credit score points when you do. The reason? Now that those accounts are paid off and closed, they are no longer included in your Length of Credit History calculation. The trick is to always keep your oldest credit card open. It's revolving credit, and unlike a loan, a revolving account doesn't automatically close when the account reaches a $0 balance. It usually remains open and available for use until the lender or the consumer (you), chooses to close it.

4. Utilization: 30%

Your utilization is how much of your credit limit you're using. For example, if you have a credit card with a $500 limit and your balance is $250, that means your utilization is 50%. That's way too high. Ideally you don't want to use more than 30% of your limits; under 20% is even better. A ratio that is too high may mean you're unable to make consistent, on-time debt payments. The higher the ratio, the higher the interest rate you might be charged on your debt and no one likes that. FYI: Your limit is calculated as an average just like your length of credit history.

Utilization Example: If you have two credit cards with the same limit ($500 each) and one of them is maxed out and has a balance of $500 and the other one isn't being used and has a $0 balance, you're utilizing 50% of your available credit.

Utilization Tip: Here's a step-by-step guide to help you figure out if you should close or keep your credit cards:

1. List ALL of your revolving credit accounts.
2. Add up your credit limits.
3. Add up your current balances.
4. Divide your balance by your credit limit.
5. Multiply your answer by 100.
6. If your current credit utilization ratio is 20% – 30% or higher, then you should not close any of your credit card accounts.

7. If your ratio is below 20%, recalculate your ratio, but do so without your newest card.
8. Keep dropping the newest card on your list until you find how many cards you can keep and still have a credit utilization rate under 30%

5. Payment History: 35%

This component of your credit score carries the most weight. Basically, it measures whether or not you pay by the due date, and whether you pay at least the minimum amount required.

Payment History Example: If your credit card bill is due every month on the 15th, by paying at least the minimum amount requested on or before the 15th, you keep this component of your credit report in good standing.

Payment History Tip: Automation is the new discipline. During Day 11 of the Challenge I encouraged you to open multiple bank accounts. One of these accounts is a Bills Account. Use your Bills Account to automate payments to your creditors. Doing so will help improve your credit history and overall credit score.

Learn Something New?
Share what you learned with me.

twitter: @thebudgetnista
Instagram: @thebudgetnista
Facebook: The Budgetnista
Forum: www.li009.liverichcrchallenge.com

Live Richer Challenge
Day 25: Interest Rates

Week 4: Credit

Today's Easy Financial Task: Lower your interest rates

How to Rock This Task :
- Choose your oldest credit card that's in good standing
- Call the customer service number on the back of the card
- Ask for a lower rate

Today I'm going to show you how to negotiate for better interest rates. Don't be fooled...you can negotiate with your credit card companies for lower interest rates. This works especially if you've had your credit cards for awhile and they're in good standing.

How to make it do what it do:
1. Go to www.MagnifyMoney.com and find a credit card with a better interest rate.
2. Choose the company of the credit card that you've had for the longest, and the one where you have the best payment history.
3. Call the customer service number on the back of that card.
4. Negotiate using the competitor you found on www.MagnifyMoney.com. Remember to be persistent and polite. No one will help you if you have a bad attitude.

Try saying something like:

"Hi_____. My name is _____. I'm calling because I just received a great offer from a different credit card company. They're offering me an introductory interest rate of only _____%.

I don't want to transfer my balance, because I've been with your company for _____ years, but I really need to lower my costs. I may have to switch cards if you can't lower the interest rate on my card with you."

They'll probably say that you already have the lowest rate they can offer you. Then you should say...

"I could pay a lot less if I transfer my balance though. I was thinking you could give me...____% as a new rate?"

If you've been late with payments or have a whole lot of debt, this may not work. But as the saying goes, a closed mouth doesn't get fed, so I'd ask anyway. Most credit card companies are not willing to lose your business to another company.

If you get your new rate, do a happy dance and make sure to get all the details. For example, is this a short-term promotional offer or your new annual percentage rate (APR)? Will the new rate go into effect immediately? What's the fine print or additional details you should be aware of, etc.?

What to do if they say no:

Yet another saying goes, if at first you don't succeed, try, try, try again. Next time ask for a supervisor. You might even have to try back in a few months, especially if your payment record isn't so clean (if you know what I mean).

Worst case scenario, you can transfer your card balance to the new card you found on www.MagnifyMoney.com. Just note that getting a new card will result in an inquiry (see Day 24 for explanation). Also, remember to keep your current card open with a small monthly charge. You'll need the years you've been with them in order to maintain your length of credit history.

Have you checked in with your accountability partners recently? You should. Practice your negotiation skills with each other before reaching out to your credit card company.

Live Richer Challenge
Day 26: Higher Score

Week 4: Credit

Today's Easy Financial Task: Raise your credit score

How to rock this task :
- Watch the Raise Your Credit Score Video
- Use the tips from the video to raise your credit score

Today's a video day! Don't you just love these days? Now that I've taught you the components of a credit score (the magic formula the credit scoring agencies use to calculate your score) and how to lower your interest rate, it's time to learn how to raise your score as much as 100 points in a year. Yup!

I know you're probably thinking, "Is it really possible to raise my credit score 100 points in only one year?" The answer is... yes! Results are not guaranteed, but I've done it and so have a bunch of my clients, students, fans, followers, and friends, based upon the steps I'm about to show you.

Before you start, let's take care of your credit cards with high interest rates that you weren't able to lower yesterday. If you haven't done so, now is the time to revisit that step.

It's video time! Get ready to learn how to raise your score quickly. Watch the Raise Your Credit Score video at www.livericherchallenge.com (Day 26: Higher Score), and meet me back here for the next steps.

If you watched the video, then this is just a review.

How to raise your score 100 points in one year...

1. Pay down debt or increase your credit limit(s). This will lower your Utilization. Utilization is 30% of your score. (revisit Day 24 for more details)
2. Pay your bills on time (payment history is 35% of your score)
3. Auto-pay off a small debt aka bring its balance to $0 EVERY month. FYI: This is where the magic happens. Doing this will make your credit score jump like Jordan. Yup! Here's how, step-by-step...

    a. Take out your credit card that has a 0$ balance. If none of your credit cards have, or are close to a $0 balance, head to www. MagnifyMoney.com and get a new card. Be mindful that applying for credit will result in an inquiry on you credit report. Inquiries stay on your report for two years and can cause your credit score to temporarily drop a few points. Don't worry, you can gain those points and more back by following these steps.

    If you're unable to qualify for an unsecured (regular) credit card, get a secured credit card. A secured card requires you to make a cash deposit that becomes your credit line for that account. For example, if you put $600 in the account, you can charge up to $600. It's easier to be approved for a secured card because it's less of a risk for the financial institution that gives it to you. The reason is that they can take your cash deposit if you don't pay off your balance.

    Looking for a secured card? First ask your bank or credit union if they offer one. If they don't offer a secured card, use www.MagnifyMoney.com to help you find the best-secured card for you.

    When looking for a secured card, make sure....

    • You're cautious of anyone that asks you for outrageous start-up fees (some places try to charge up to $200) or ask you to call a 1-900 number that will charge you money.

• You're sure to ask if your transactions will be reported to all three major credit bureaus. You want them to see that you're paying off your debts so your score can begin to improve.

• You understand that some banks might force you to wait for a year after you've filed bankruptcy to get a secured card. If that's the case, focus on building up your savings in the meantime.

• You get a secured card at a bank you want to continue to use for a while. After months of on-time payments, you'll eventually want to ask if you can switch to an unsecured (regular) card with the same bank, so choose wisely.

b. Pay off your balance every month: Something magically happens when you pay a debt off in full each month. Your credit score does a happy-dance and jumps up. It doesn't matter if the debt you paid off was $5000 or $5, same happy dance occurs. You can encourage your credit score to do a happy dance 12 times a year, by paying off your credit card in full every month.

Do this by placing a small automatic payment on your $0 balance card each month (ie: magazine subscription, gym membership, phone bill). That bill should be the ONLY thing this card is used for. Then, sign-up for automatic bill-pay at your bank (this should be a free service), and instruct the bank to send the full payment of your bill, from your BILLS Account (Day 11), to your credit card every month. This will create a payment loop effect that eliminates the flawed human element....you. I suggest you leave this credit card at home and allow the loop to work for you without interference.

4. Become an authorized user on a credit card account in good standing

The Good News:

When you're added as an authorized user, the account will appear on your credit reports too. If the account remains positive with a low balance, it can help you establish and improve your credit history.

The Great News:

An authorized user has permission to use the credit card, but is not responsible for any of the debt.

The Awesome News:

If the account is reported and there are delinquencies, it's possible that the delinquencies are affecting your scores too. However, because you're not responsible for the debt, credit scoring companies will remove authorized user accounts that become delinquent. The account will most likely be removed automatically, but if you find it is still being reported, follow the dispute instructions provided with your credit reports and request that it be deleted.

Basically, the authorized user gets all of the benefits and none of the risks. How great is that? If you're a parent with great credit, this is a good way to help your kids establish credit without the risks involved by giving them an actual credit card.

What do you think? Can you see your score jumping like Jordan now?

Today's task is so useful I want you to share it. Repost the video on your social media networks and help someone else LIVE RICHER.

Live Richer Challenge
Day 27: Credit Clean-up

Week 4: Credit

Today's Easy Financial Task: Clean up your credit report

How to rock this task :
- Take out your free credit reports from Day 22
- Dispute incorrect information on your reports

Today we'll get your credit report cleaned up. What should you look for when cleaning up your credit report?

1. Check to make sure your name, address, and basic information are correct.
2. Look for any additional, incorrect information. For example, are there any accounts you don't recognize? Is there a debt you paid off, yet it's still being reported as outstanding? Maybe it says you were late on a payment but you weren't.
3. Look for any negative history over seven years old because it should have fallen off unless it's a bankruptcy, judgement, tax lien, or foreclosure. These items can stay on your report for ten years.

How to address the issues on your credit report:
1. Do an online search for the mailing address of the credit bureau(s) you're writing to.
2. Write a letter to the bureau stating what information you think is wrong. Once you do so, the creditor must investigate the item(s) within 30 days, unless it considers your dispute frivolous. Get a Dispute Letter template for free at www.livericherchallenge.com. Find it under Day 22: Credit Clean-Up.
3. Include copies of your proof, i.e. complete name, address, social

security number, copy of paid bills.

4. Clearly identify each item in your report that you're disputing, state the facts, explain why you're disputing, then request a deletion or correction. Enclose a copy of your credit report with the questionable items clearly marked.
5. Send your letter via certified mail, return receipt requested, and keep copies.
6. **Never use the online dispute option.** By doing so, you may be giving up your rights to re-dispute an item should it not be decided in your favor. Sometimes there's small print on the agreement that doesn't allow you to re-dispute - another instance where it's important to read the fine print!

When the dispute is answered, make sure to follow up.

If you request that a change be made and the credit bureau complies, they will send you an updated copy of your credit report. Also ask that they send a correction notice to any entity that accessed your credit report in the last six months.

Make sure to check your other credit reports to ensure that corrective action is taken there as well. The three main credit bureaus communicate with each other electronically, so a correction made on one report should be reflected on the other versions too, but check to make sure.

What to do if your dispute is denied:
• Credit bureaus MUST make sure that the information they report is verifiable upon your request (within 15 days from the date they conclude their investigation).
• If you ask, they have to provide the method of verification: name, address, and phone number of the company that provided the verification, as well as proof that they received the original dated contract with your signature on it.
• If they cannot provide this information, they must remove the item from your report.

Most credit bureaus aren't willing to go through this much trouble or are unable to provide this information and will instead correct the item you're disputing.

Now get to it! Your new and improved credit report awaits.

If you need more help, here's an awesome resource: "What the FICO: 12 Steps to Repairing Your Credit" by Ash Cash

Live Richer Challenge
Day 28: Review, Reflect, Relax

Week 4: Credit

Today's Easy Financial Task: Review, Reflect, Relax

How to Rock This Task:
- *Review* this week's LIVE RICHER Challenge tasks
- *Reflect* on the changes you've made to your credit situation
- *Relax.* Tomorrow we start Week 5's theme: Insurance & Investing!

Congrats! It's the end of week 4 of the LIVE RICHER Challenge. We've covered Money Mindset, Budgeting & Savings, Debt, and now Credit.

It's time for another break day. Today I want you to: Review, Reflect, and Relax. It's also a great day to catch up on any of the tasks you still have to complete.

Feel free to share with me what you've learned over the last four weeks by doing this challenge.

Don't forget to share what you've learned with your accountability partner.

Tomorrow begins Week 5 and it's all about Insurance and Investing.

Week 4: Credit Recap Checklist

○ **Day 22:** Easy Financial Task: Get your free Credit Report(s)

○ **Day 23:** Easy Financial Task: Get your free Credit Score(s)

○ **Day 24:** Easy Financial Task: Learn how your Credit Score is calculated

○ **Day 25:** Easy Financial Task: Lower your interest rates

○ **Day 26:** Easy Financial Task: Raise your Credit Score

○ **Day 27:** Easy Financial Task: Clean up your Credit Report

○ **Day 28:** Easy Financial Task: Review, Reflect, Relax

Week 4 Reflections

WEEK 5: INSURANCE & INVESTING

THIS WEEK'S GOAL:

INSURANCE: To fully understand your insurance plans and to make adjustments for more, less, or different insurance coverage based upon your personal needs.

INVESTING: To determine where you currently stand in relation to retirement and wealth accumulation. To define investment goals and the steps that need to be taken to achieve those goals.

Live Richer Challenge
Day 29: Policy Review

Week 5: Insurance & Investing

Today's Easy Financial Task: Review your policy

How to Rock This Task :
- Take out and review your insurance policies
- Note your deductible, total coverage, premium, discounts, and events covered

Woop woop, you've made it to Week 5: Insurance & Investing week! This week I'll show you how to make sure you're properly insured and I'll help you to begin achieving your investment goals.

Let's begin with insurance.

It's time to take out your car, home, life, health, disability insurance, etc. Some of the things you're going to look for are:

Deductible: The amount you must pay out of pocket before your insurance will pay any expenses.

Total Coverage: How much protection your policy covers.

Premium: The amount of money you pay for your insurance coverage each month, quarter, or year.

Discounts: Specials deals that your insurance company offers, i.e. accident free, alumni, or workplace discounts.

Events covered: The type of situations your insurance may or may not cover. For example, homeowners insurance doesn't necessarily cover flood damage, but could cover fire damage.

Getting to know your current policies is important and will save you money and frustration when it's time for you to make a claim.

My policies... (include the deductible, total coverage, premium, discounts and events covered)

Live Richer Challenge
Day 30: Competitor Quotes

Week 5: Insurance & Investing

Today's Easy Financial Task: Get quotes from competitors

How to rock this task:
- Take out your current policies
- Make a list of your policy competitors
- Ask for quotes using the stats from your current policies

Today I'm going to show you how to gain the leverage you'll need to negotiate lower insurance rates with your current providers.

The first step is to get competitive rates for the same or better coverage. Do this by making a list of competitors you want to contact. Then take out your current policies and call new companies to ask if they can offer you a better price than your current premium.

Remember: Don't sacrifice coverage for a cheaper rate. You want them to offer your current coverage for a cheaper premium.

Keep this in mind: If you share your social security number with the company when asking for a quote, doing so will trigger an inquiry on your credit report. Inquiries stay on your credit report for two years and can temporarily lower your credit score. So don't go crazy asking for quotes, although it's still worth it to check for policies like home and car, because saving thousands of dollars is worth losing 10 points off your credit score.

My policy competitors and their rates...

Live Richer Challenge
Day 31: Negotiate

Week 5: Insurance & Investing

Today's Easy Financial Task: Ask your providers for discounts

How to Rock This Task:
- Take out the list of your policy's competitors' rates from yesterday's task
- Call your current providers and negotiate using competitive rates as leverage

Cha Ching! That's the sound of the money you'll save once you call to negotiate new rates on your policies.

Now that you've got a list of competitive rates from other insurance companies, you can reach out to your current companies and ask for discounts. Use the competitive rates as a bargaining tool. Worst case scenario: your company denies your request and then you make a switch. However, it's in your insurance company's best interest to keep you, so it's likely you'll come out on top.

Practice your negotiation skills with your accountability partner. If you get a company to lower your rate, share your success and method with your partner.

I can't wait to hear your success stories. Share them with me here:

Twitter: @thebudgetnista
Instagram: @thebudgetnista
Facebook: The Budgetnista
Forum: www.livericherchallenge.com

Live Richer Challenge
Day 32: Knowledge is Money

Week 5: Insurance & Investing

Today's Easy Financial Task: Get educated

How to Rock This Task:
- Define key investment terms
- Identify investment sites and resources

Now on to investing. Investing is the only way to gain real wealth, so let's get to it. A rich investor is an educated investor. Here are a few key terms to get you started:

Net worth - A measure of your monetary value. Your total assets (things that put money into your pocket), minus your total liabilities (things that take money out of your pocket).

Assets - Anything that adds value and increases your net worth, ie. a home (usually), art (possibly), stocks, business, etc.

Liabilities - Anything that loses value and decreases your net worth, ie. a car, electronics, clothes, those designer shoes (real or fake -they still decrease in value).

Interest Rate - A rate which is charged or paid for the use of money. Interest rates go both ways: if you're borrowing money it will cost you, if you're lending money (i.e. CDs, savings accounts, etc.) you make money.

Stock - A share in a public company that, when purchased, makes you part owner.

Shareholder - An owner of shares (or stocks) in a company.

Dividend - Money paid regularly by a company to its shareholders out of its profits.

Mutual Fund - Funds that include a group of stocks, bonds, or other investments. Unlike a stock where you purchase one company at a time, with mutual funds you purchase a group of investments based on your investment goals.

Bonds - An IOU from a company or municipality. You lend them money by purchasing their bond and they owe you back according to the terms of the contract.

Traditional IRA vs. Roth IRA - An IRA is an **I**ndividual **R**etirement **A**ccount. The main difference between the two has to do with the income tax on the money you put into the plans. With a **Traditional IRA**, you pay the taxes when you withdraw the money at and during retirement. With a **Roth IRA**, it's the exact opposite and you pay the taxes on the front end, but there are no taxes to pay once you retire. In both Traditional and Roth IRAs, your money grows, tax free, while it's in the account.

401k - A savings plan that allows employees to contribute a fixed amount of income to a retirement account and defer taxes until withdrawal.

Get even more terms and resources from sites like www.investopedia.com and www.learnvest.com.

Now that you know some key investment terms and have some site resources, tomorrow we'll identify your investment goals.

Live Richer Challenge
Day 33: Investment Goals

Week 5: Insurance & Investing

Today's Easy Financial Task: Identify investment goals and current investments

How to Rock This Task:
- Identify your investment goals. Use a retirement calendar to help
- Take out and review the investments that you currently have

Now that you've gotten comfortable with some investment definitions, let's identify your investment goals and review your current investments.

Yay, it's another video day! Go to www.livericherchallenge.com (Day 33: Investment Goals) to watch me share my best investing goal-setting strategies. In this week's video, I share how to define your risk tolerance, and your investing: why, when, what and how.

The most important part of investing is setting a goal. Without one you won't know what to work towards or how to measure success. An easy way to establish a goal is by using a retirement calculator to discover exactly how much you need to invest to retire comfortably. Try the calculator at www.livericherchallenge.com under Day 33: Your Investment Goals.

Once you've identify how much you'll need to retire, take out and review your portfolio. Don't know what you're looking at? That's okay, make a list of questions that you have because tomorrow we'll start to get them answered. Some of the things you should be looking for are:

1. How much money you have invested.
2. How well your investments are doing.
3. Your investment allocations.
4. Your investment risk-tolerance (conservative, moderate, or aggressive).

If you don't have any investments, don't panic. Now's a great time to start. Tomorrow I'll show you how to get professional help to get you up and running.

Live Richer Challenge
Day 34: Live Help

Week 5: Insurance & Investing

Today's Easy Financial Task: Talk to a financial advisor

How to Rock This Task:
- Gather the retirement investing options from your job
- If you don't have a workplace retirement plan, choose two investment vehicles you're interested in learning more about
- Learn how to find a qualified financial advisor and make an appointment

Now that have your investment goals, it's time to reach out to a professional for help. Choosing the right financial advisor is as important as choosing a doctor, mechanic, or childcare provider. Not only are you looking for someone who's knowledgeable, you're also looking for someone with whom you can build a good relationship. You should like them-- after all you'll be sharing intimate financial details with them.

Once you gather your current or desired investment material, it's time to find a qualified financial advisor. Not sure how? If your investments are through your job, you likely have an assigned advisor. Ask your Human Resource Department or check your statement for contact information.

If you don't have work related investments, the best place to find an advisor is through your family, friends, and co-workers. Is there anyone you know whose retirement and investment plan you admire? Start with your accountability partners. Reach out to them and ask who helped them. Once you have at least two referrals, it's time to interview your prospects.

According to Forbes, here are the ten questions you should ask your potential financial advisor:

1. Are you a fiduciary?

   A fiduciary is a person who has to place the client's interest ahead of his or her own. Fiduciaries must also disclose what their fees are, how they're compensated, and any other conflicts or potential conflicts of interest that might influence an individual's decision to use their services. (Forbes)
2. How much are your services, and you do you charge for them?
3. What licenses, credentials, or other certifications do you have?
5. What types of clients do you specialize in?
6. Could I see a sample financial plan?
7. What is your investment approach?
8. How much contact do you have with your clients?
9. Will I be working only with you or with a team?
10. What makes your client experience unique?

Remember, the way to truly gain wealth is through investing, so make sure you start today by getting professional help.

Live Richer Challenge
Day 35: Review, Reflect, Relax

Week 5: Insurance & Investing

Today's Easy Financial Task: Review, Reflect, Relax

How to Rock This Task:
- *Review* this week's LIVE RICHER Challenge tasks
- *Reflect* on the changes you've made to your insurance and investing situation
- *Relax.* You completed the challenge!

Congrats! You're almost the end of the LIVE RICHER Challenge. How do you feel? You should should feel like a rock star.

Now you have a new money mindset, a budget, savings, debt, credit, insurance, and investment plan. How cool is that?

All I want you to do today is: Review, Reflect, Relax, and celebrate with your accountability partners. Today is also a great day to catch up on any of the tasks you still have to complete.

Feel free to share with me what you've learned by doing this challenge over the last five weeks. Also share what you've learned with someone who needs help getting on financial track.

I can't wait to hear how this experience helped you. Tell me here:

Twitter: @thebudgetnista
Instagram: @thebudgetnista
Facebook: The Budgetnista
Forum: www.livericherchallenge.com

Week 5: Insurance & Investing Recap Checklist

○ **Day 29:** Easy Financial Task: Review your policy

○ **Day 30:** Easy Financial Task: Get quotes from competitors

○ **Day 31:** Easy Financial Task: Ask your providers for discounts

○ **Day 32:** Easy Financial Task: Get educated

○ **Day 33:** Easy Financial Task: Identify investment goals and current investments

○ **Day 34:** Easy Financial Task: Talk to a financial advisor

○ **Day 35:** Easy Financial Task: Review, Reflect, Relax

Week 5 Reflections

_____

_____

_____

_____

_____

_____

_____

_____

DAY 36: LIVE RICHER

FINAL DAY'S GOAL:

To learn how to purposefully & passionately pursue your ideal life, using your finances as one of your tools.

Live Richer Challenge
Day 36: LIVE RICHER

Final Day: LIVE RICHER

Today's Easy Financial Task: Give Back and LIVE RICHER

How to rock this task:
- Create a vision board
- Give back

Now that you've completed the LIVE RICHER Challenge, it's time to begin looking at its effects on your whole life.

Remember, money is never the end goal. It's merely a tool to help you get what you want and need in order to LIVE RICHER. To LIVE RICHER means to purposefully and passionately pursue your ideal life.

What does an ideal life look like for you? What awesomeness have you always dreamed of experiencing? The key is to use your money as a tool to make that experience happen.

Today's task is to find what your richer life looks, feels, tastes, and smells like. I also want you to begin to plan how you'll use what you've learned as a result of the LIVE RICHER Challenge. One of the best ways to do this is by creating a vision board. Not sure how to make a vision board? Head on over to www.livericherchallenge.com (Day 36: LIVE RICHER) for details.

Although the LIVE RICHER Challenge is complete, your richer life has just begun. Don't be a stranger. I'd love to hear what you're thinking and feeling now that we've reached the end. Please share your success story with me at tiffany@thebudgetnista.com.

One last thing... Giving activates abundance. It's great to be helped; it's even greater to use what you've been given to help someone else. Spread the wealth by sharing your time, energy, finances, and knowledge with those who have less than you.

LIVE RICHER,
Tiffany "The Budgetnista" Aliche

Live Richer Challenge Recap Checklist

○ **Week 1:** I completed my Money Mindset tasks

○ **Week 2:** I completed my Budgeting & Saving tasks

○ **Week 3:** I completed my Debt tasks

○ **Week 4:** I completed my Credit tasks

○ **Week 5:** I completed my Insurance & Investing tasks

○ **Day 36:** I am actively working toward LIVING a RICHER life

LIVE RICHER Challenge Reflections

_____

_____

_____

_____

_____

_____

_____

_____

_____

_____

_____

Acknowledgments:

First and foremost, I would like to give my most grateful thanks to God. He always blesses us. It is we who allow or do not allow our blessings to manifest.

I also want to thank Mommy, Daddy, and my sisters: Karen, Tracy, Carol, and Lisa. You are my cheerleaders, my best friends, my sounding board, and my inspiration. Anyone who knows the *Aliche Girls* knows how supportive we are of each other. Thank you.

To all my family, both here and abroad, thank you for your constant love and support. The strong foundation you've provided is the reason I've been able to reach such heights.

Taylor Medine and Marne Benson, thank you so much for helping me transform and polish my words into a book I can be proud of.

Jerrell, thank you for your unwavering support and love.

Thank you to my designers, Baja Ukweli, Ashly Nash and Hector Torres. I came to you at crunch time and you more than delivered.

Thank you Sierra Kirby. I literally could not have launched the LIVE RICHER Challenge without you.

Special thanks to Linda Iferika, Dreena Whitfield, all my family, friends, co-workers, and all of my well wishers.

Lastly, I especially want to thank you. Yes, you reading these words. You allowed me to help you LIVE RICHER. You gave me more than I ever gave you. I am forever grateful.

Tiffany 'The Budgetnista' Aliche, a New Jersey native, earned a Bachelor's Degree in Business Administration from Montclair State University. She forwent a career in corporate America to teach undeserved youth in Newark, NJ and went on to continue her graduate studies at Seton Hall University.

Tiffany is an award-winning teacher of financial empowerment, and is quickly becoming America's favorite financial educator. The Budgetnista specializes in the delivery of financial literacy, and has served as the personal finance education expert for City National Bank.

Since 2008, The Budgetnista has been a brand ambassador and spokesperson for a number of organizations - delivering financial education through seminars, workshops, curricula and trainings.

Author of #1 Amazon bestseller, The One Week Budget, Tiffany and her financial advice have been featured in The New York Times, Reuters, US News and World Report, the TODAY show, PBS, Fox Business, MSNBC, CBS MoneyWatch, TIME, ESSENCE Magazine, and FORBES. She regularly blogs about personal finance for The Huffington Post.

Learn more about Tiffany and The Budgetnista here: thebudgetnista.com

39092 09434344 1

Made in the USA
San Bernardino, CA
13 January 2016